Watch It Grow
Duck
Barrie Watts

Smart Apple Media

First published in 2002 by Franklin Watts
96 Leonard Street, London EC2A 4XD, United Kingdom
Franklin Watts Australia, 56 O'Riordan Street, Alexandria, NSW 2015
Copyright © 2002 Barrie Watts

Editor: Adrian Cole, Art director: Jonathan Hair, Photographer: Barrie Watts, Illustrator: David Burroughs, Consultant: Beverley Mathias, REACH

Published in the United States by Smart Apple Media
1980 Lookout Drive, North Mankato, Minnesota 56003

U.S. publication copyright © 2003 Smart Apple Media
International copyright reserved in all countries. No part of this book may be reproduced in any form without written permission from the publisher.
Printed in Hong Kong

Library of Congress Cataloging-in-Publication Data

Watts, Barrie. Duck / Barrie Watts. p. cm. — (Watch it grow)
Summary: A simple introduction to the physical characteristics and behavior of ducks, emphasizing the birth and development of ducklings.
ISBN 1-58340-197-0 1. Ducks—Life cycles—Juvenile literature.
[1. Ducks. 2. Animals—Infancy.] I. Title.
QL696.A52 W42 2002 598.4'1—dc21 2002017032

2 4 6 8 9 7 5 3

How to use this book

Watch It Grow has been specially designed to cater to a range of reading and learning abilities. Initially, children may just follow the pictures. Ask them to describe in their own words what they see. Other children will enjoy reading the single sentence in large type in conjunction with the pictures. This single sentence is then expanded in the main text. More adept readers will be able to follow the text and pictures by themselves through to the conclusion of the duck's life cycle.

Contents

Ducks come from eggs.

Here is a white duck egg at its actual size. It is about the same size as a large chicken egg.

Duck eggs have a hard shell and are filled with **yolk** and white.

During the spring, a female duck may lay about 15 eggs in her nest.

She uses feathers from her body to line the nest. Next, the duck **incubates** the eggs. The warmth of her body helps a tiny duckling grow inside each egg.

The egg hatches.

After about 28 days, the duckling begins to hatch. It uses the hard tip of its bill to break the tough skin that covers the inside of the shell.

Slowly, the egg cracks and
pieces of shell fall away.
The duckling can breathe air
for the first time in its life.

The duckling breaks out.

It takes up to 48 hours for the duckling to break out of the egg completely. It is tired and its feathers are wet. The duckling's mother keeps it warm until its feathers dry out.

The duckling still has some of the egg **yolk** in its body. Over the next few days it will use the yolk for food, until it is strong enough to find something to eat.

The feathers are dry.

Two hours after hatching, the duckling is dry. Its fluffy feathers are called **down**. The down keeps the duckling warm, but it is not **waterproof**.

If the duckling gets cold and wet it could die, so it stays in the safe nest. The duckling sleeps and rests in the nest for about four days.

The duckling gets stronger.

After four days, the duckling's legs are strong enough for it to walk without falling over. It has used up all the **yolk** in its body and is very hungry.

The duckling flaps its stumpy wings to make them stronger. But it will have to wait until it grows its adult feathers before it can fly.

The duckling swims.

The duckling takes its first
swim with its mother. It stays
very close to her. The duckling
loves being in the water.

It will spend more time each day swimming, feeding, and washing itself. Even though it can swim easily with its **webbed feet**, the duckling at this age cannot stay in the cold water for too long. Its **down** will get too wet.

The duckling feeds.

The duckling eats water weeds and other plants. As it swims, it also looks for food under the water. Its eyes are protected by a thin layer of skin.

The duckling also eats seeds and anything else that looks like food.

If it eats something **inedible**, like a twig, the duckling spits it out. The duckling needs to eat a lot every day to keep growing and stay healthy.

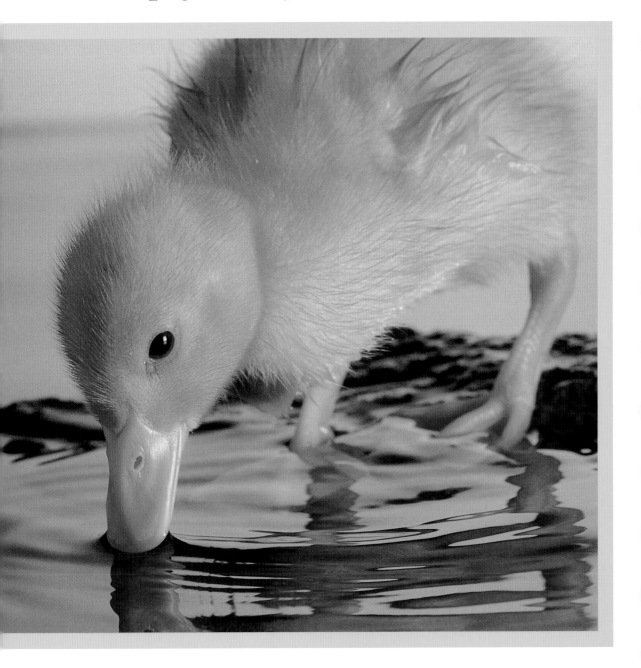

The duckling goes for a walk.

The duckling also looks for food on land. It eats grass and crawling insects.

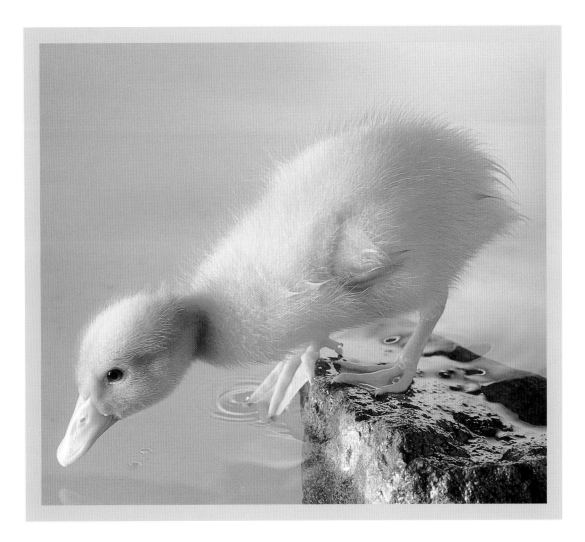

The duckling's legs are stronger, but it still needs to rest during the day. It usually returns to the water when it is tired. It is safer there than on land, where it might be eaten by **predators**.

The duckling cleans itself.

The duckling washes by splashing water over its body. As soon as it comes out of the water, it **preens** itself.

It checks the fluffy **down** with its bill to make sure that it is clean.
The down must be kept in good condition to keep the duckling warm.

The duckling's bill changes.

After three weeks, the duckling's bill has doubled in size. The bill is made from a tough material similar to that of human fingernails.

The bill hardens and changes color as the duckling grows older. Inside the bill are tiny, soft teeth. These help the duckling to grip slippery water weeds and tear tough grass.

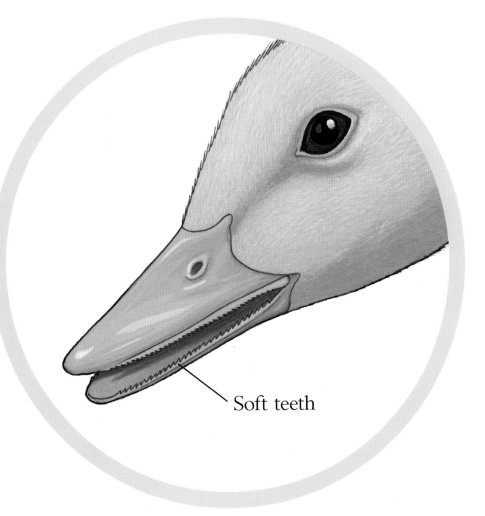

Soft teeth

The adult feathers grow.

When it is a month old, the duckling starts to grow its white adult feathers. They are made of a material called **keratin**. They push out some of the fluffy **down**.

The down closest to the duckling's body is not pushed out. It remains and helps the duckling to stay warm.

As the duckling grows older, it will shed its feathers several times. This is called **molting**.

The duck flaps its wings.

Three months after hatching, the duck is almost fully grown. Soon it will be able to fly. However, its wing muscles are not strong enough yet.

The duck flaps its wings to exercise the muscles and make them stronger.

Throughout the winter ducks live together. They feed and try to survive the cold weather.

The adult ducks mate.

The following spring, the adult duck looks for a partner with whom to mate. After mating, the female duck makes a nest from dried grass, leaves, and fluffy **down**.

She lays her eggs in the nest
and then **incubates** them.
Four weeks later, ducklings
will hatch.

Word bank

Down - the soft, fluffy feathers that cover the body of a duckling and keep it warm. Even when a duckling gets adult feathers it will still keep some of its down.

Incubates - when a bird sits on its eggs to keep them warm so they will hatch.

Inedible - something that cannot be eaten, such as a twig or stone.

Keratin - the material from which feathers are made. It is flexible and light in weight.

Molting - when a bird sheds its feathers.

Predators - animals that hunt and eat other animals. A fox is a duck's main predator.

Preens - when a bird cleans its feathers with its bill to keep them healthy and straight.

Waterproof - when water cannot pass through something. The down of a duckling is not waterproof.

Webbed feet - feet that have toes that are joined together by thin pieces of skin.

Yolk - the food in an egg that is eaten by a duckling when it is very young.

Life cycle

After about 28 days, the duckling uses its bill to crack open the shell of its egg.

Next spring, after mating, the female duck lays its own eggs.

The duckling breaks out. It is tired and wet.

After three months, the duck is almost fully grown.

After four days, the duckling can walk and swim.

One month after hatching, the duckling grows adult feathers.

The duckling looks for crawling insects to eat.

After three weeks, the duckling's bill is larger and stronger.

Index